SAM SHEPARD

The God of Hell

Sam Shepard is the Pulitzer Prize–winning author of more than forty-five plays. He was a finalist for the W. H. Smith Literary Award for his story collection *Great Dream of Heaven*, and he has also written the story collection *Cruising Paradise*, two collections of prose pieces, *Motel Chronicles* and *Hawk Moon*, and *Rolling Thunder Logbook*, a diary of Bob Dylan's 1975 Rolling Thunder Review tour. As an actor he has appeared in more than thirty films, and he received an Oscar nomination in 1984 for his performance in *The Right Stuff*. His screenplay for *Paris, Texas* won the Grand Jury Prize at the 1984 Cannes Film Festival, and he wrote and directed the film *Far North* in 1988. Shepard's plays, eleven of which have won Obie Awards, include *Buried Child*, *The Late Henry Moss*, *Simpatico*, *Curse of the Starving Class*, *True West*, *Fool for Love*, and *A Lie of the Mind*, which won a New York Drama Desk Award. A member of the American Academy of Arts and Letters, Shepard received the Gold Medal for Drama from the Academy in 1992, and in 1994 he was inducted into the Theatre Hall of Fame.

The God of Hell

SAM SHEPARD

The God of Hell

A PLAY

VINTAGE BOOKS

A Division of Random House, Inc.

New York

A VINTAGE ORIGINAL, APRIL 2005

Copyright © 2005 by Sam Shepard

Vintage and colophon are registered trademarks
of Random House, Inc.

Library of Congress Cataloging-in-Publication Data
Shepard, Sam, 1943–
The god of hell : a play / Sam Shepard.
p.   cm.
"A Vintage original"—T.p. verso.
ISBN 1-4000-9651-0
1. Liberty—Drama.   2. Conservatism—Drama.   3. Right and left
(Political science)—Drama.   4. Middle West—Drama.   5. Political
plays.   I. Title.
PS3569.H394 G63 2005
812'.54—dc22
2004065122

Book design by Rebecca Aidlin

www.vintagebooks.com

Printed in the United States of America
10 9 8 7 6 5 4 3 2

The God of Hell premiered in New York City at the Actors Studio Drama School Theater on October 28, 2004. Produced by New School University, Bob Kerry, President; Arjun Appadurai, Provost; Evangeline Morphos and Jack O'Connor, Producers. The cast was as follows:

FRANK	Randy Quaid
WELCH	Tim Roth
EMMA	J. Smith-Cameron
HAYNES	Frank Wood

Directed by Lou Jacob
Designed by David Korins
Costumes by Ilona Somogyi
Lighting by David Lander
Original music and sound design by Lindsay Jones
Fight direction by J. Allen Suddeth
Production managed by Jared Clarkin
Production stage managed by Linda Marvel

The God of Hell

Scene One

Set: Early morning. Interior, very simple Midwestern farmhouse. Frosty windows looking out to distant vague, snowbound pastures— no details. Two rooms separated by a simple kitchen counter. Small kitchen stage left with faded linoleum floor. Modest living room, stage right, with plank wood floor; small couch downstage right. Many potted plants of various sizes line the walls of the living room, not arranged with any sense of design or order. An exterior door upstage right leading out to a small mudroom and porch landing. A black cast-iron school bell hangs from the porch ceiling on a short rope. Stage left wall of kitchen has an open arched entranceway leading to other rooms dimly lit offstage. The usual kitchen appliances, cupboards, and sink—all dating from the fifties. Down left corner of kitchen is a semiconcealed staircase leading down to the basement, dim yellow light leaking up from stairs. Handrail and first flight of stairs leading down are all that's visible to the audience.

Lights up on EMMA *in blue terry-cloth bathrobe, slippers, moving methodically back and forth from the kitchen sink, where she fills a yellow plastic pitcher with water and carries it to the plants. She*

waters plants and returns to refill pitcher, then repeats the process.
FRANK, *her husband, sits on couch with pair of work boots in his lap, greasing them with mink oil. It's a while before they speak.*

EMMA: He's not up yet?

FRANK: Haven't heard him.

EMMA: I thought they were supposed to be early risers.

FRANK: Who?

EMMA: These scientists.

FRANK: He's not a scientist. What made you think that?

EMMA: I thought you said he was a scientist.

FRANK: Nope.

EMMA: Well, what is he then?

FRANK: I'm not sure. I mean, I'm not sure about his official title.

EMMA: Official? So, he's working for the government or something?

FRANK: I think he's in research.

EMMA: I thought you said it was something to do with the government.

FRANK: No, I don't think I said that.

EMMA: Arms or something.

FRANK: Arms?

EMMA: Munitions.

FRANK: I don't know. It has initials.

EMMA: What does?

FRANK: The outfit he works for. Out there in Colorado. DMDS or SSCI or something like that. You know how everything has initials now.

EMMA: DMDS or SSCI? Is that what you said?

FRANK: Something like that.

EMMA: What the heck is that? What does that stand for?

FRANK: I have no idea, Emma. I wasn't really following it. He was kind of panicky on the phone.

EMMA: Panicky?

FRANK: Yes. Panicky. Breathless. Like he was in a rush.

EMMA: Running?

FRANK: What?

EMMA: Running away from something, maybe?

FRANK: No—just—flustered.

EMMA: Oh, flustered. That's different. Flustered.

(*Pause. She continues watering.*)

Well, how come I haven't met him before this? He's such an old friend of yours, supposedly.

FRANK: Supposedly? There's no "supposedly" about it.

EMMA: Well, how come you've hardly ever mentioned him?

FRANK: I don't know. He kind of disappeared for a while. I thought he was dead, actually.

EMMA: Dead?

FRANK: Yeah—or missing.

EMMA: Really?

FRANK: Yeah—or tortured even.

EMMA: Tortured? My God!

FRANK: Maybe.

EMMA: What kind of research is he involved in where he gets tortured?

FRANK: I didn't say he was tortured. I said, I thought he might have been —he could have been.

EMMA: Well, that's kinda serious, isn't it? I mean, tortured—criminy!

FRANK: He said it was all top secret.

EMMA: Oh—so that's why you're not telling me then.

FRANK: No, no—I'm telling you as much as he told me, Emma. It's just that—

EMMA: You don't get tortured unless you know something or somebody thinks you know something.

FRANK: No—yeah, well, he probably wasn't tortured then.

EMMA: You were exaggerating.

FRANK: No! I really don't know anything about it, Emma. I didn't want to stick my nose into his business. He just said that the bottom had fallen out and he needed a place to stay. That's all he told me.

EMMA: What bottom was he referring to?

FRANK: See, there you go again.

EMMA: There I go again, what?

FRANK: Sticking your nose into his business.

EMMA: I don't know this man.

FRANK: He's a friend of mine. I told you.

EMMA: I don't know anything about him. He could be hiding, as far as I know.

FRANK: Hiding? What would he be hiding from?

EMMA: How should I know? He's *your* friend.

(FRANK *puts his boots on and stands.*)

FRANK: I'm going down to feed the heifers.

EMMA: How long's he going to stay here, Frank?

FRANK: Long as he needs to.

EMMA: I'll start the bacon.

FRANK: Good.

EMMA: Should I wake him up?

FRANK: I wouldn't.

EMMA: Maybe he'd like some bacon.

FRANK: You never know. (*short pause*) You're going to drown those plants.

(FRANK *exits.* EMMA *alone—stares out window as* FRANK *crosses, outside. He waves to her. She blows him a kiss. She crosses to the kitchen, dumps the empty pitcher into the sink. It rattles around. She goes to the stove, turns on a burner, sets frying pan on it. She goes to the fridge, takes out bacon, peels off slices. She crosses to top of basement staircase landing, stops, and yells down to their unseen guest, the bacon strips hanging from her hand.*)

EMMA: Mr. Haynes? Are you up yet, Mr. Haynes?

(*No answer. She goes to the stove and slaps bacon into the frying pan. She turns fire down slightly. Suddenly, the doorbell rings: a very loud, old-fashioned, crank-style doorbell with a rasping, brittle sound.* EMMA *turns abruptly toward door, very surprised. She pauses a moment, as though wondering if she imagined it; then the doorbell rings again—longer and more persistent this time. She picks up a dishtowel and wipes her hands as she crosses to door. She opens door, which swings downstage, blocking the audience's view of who is standing there. A man's arm pops into view, dangling a large cookie in the shape of an American flag, with red, white, and blue frosting.* EMMA *jumps back. A male voice is heard from behind door.)*

MALE VOICE: Cookie? American made. Oat and raisin. Totally organic—even the frosting.

(EMMA *just stares bewilderedly at the cookie dangling from the hand.)*

EMMA: No—uh—what is it? What—we don't—need anything.

(WELCH *steps into the room, quickly closing the door behind him.* EMMA *backs up a little, holding the dishrag to her chest.* WELCH—*dark suit with American flag pin in his lapel, short cropped hair, crisp white shirt, red tie, attaché case in one hand and the cookie in the other. Big grin.)*

WELCH: *(offering cookie)* American-made cookie? One of the best you ever tasted. Guaranteed. Take a bite.

EMMA: No—thank you.

WELCH: Hold it then. Just take ahold of it and feel its wonderful weight and texture.

EMMA: No—I'm sorry, but—we're not interested.

WELCH: Not interested—not at all interested.

EMMA: In cookies—

WELCH: Aah—

(WELCH *bites into the cookie himself and savors it, smiling broadly at* EMMA. EMMA *stares back as* WELCH *crunches.*)

EMMA: Did you, uh—come to see my husband or something? Who exactly are you?

WELCH: Your husband. That's him, down below in the barn, I take it. Mumbling to the cows. Riding around on the tractor like a little boy. A child of the plains.

EMMA: Yes. That's him. And he's not a little boy. He's a big man.

WELCH: He looks pretty American, doesn't he?

EMMA: I beg your pardon?

WELCH: I mean—descent—hereditary-wise. Authentic! He looks authentic, is what I'm driving at. He could fool somebody.

EMMA: Fool?

WELCH: Hard to tell from a distance, of course. Easy to make snap judgments. He could be one of those middle Europeans or something. Latvian maybe. Belarusian.

EMMA: I think you must have the wrong house or something. I don't know what in the world—

(WELCH *suddenly moves very quickly across to the kitchen cupboards.* EMMA *just stands there, watching.*)

WELCH: Would you mind if I borrow a saucer? I don't want to get crumbs all over your floor. I can see you run a very tight ship here.

(WELCH *sets his case down on kitchen counter, opens cupboard, and takes out a white saucer. He places the cookie on it and notices the bacon on stove.*)

Bacon's burning.

EMMA: Oh—

WELCH: I've got it.

(*He turns off burner under skillet.*)

EMMA: Thank you.

(EMMA *stands still, in semishock.* WELCH *turns to her, still munching cookie. He surveys kitchen.*)

WELCH: This is Wisconsin, isn't it? I'm not mistaken about that. I must have crossed the border by now. I'm sure of it.

EMMA: Border?

WELCH: Wisconsin. The Wisconsin-Minnesota border.

EMMA: Oh—I thought you meant—

WELCH: I'm traveling from west to east.

EMMA: Oh—I see. Yes. This is.

WELCH: What?

EMMA: Wisconsin.

WELCH: Yes. I was pretty sure of that. I was traveling from east to west before, but now I'm reversing. Like Lewis and Clark. You remember them?

EMMA: Who?

WELCH: The Department keeps me on my toes.

EMMA: Department?

WELCH: Yes. The Mighty Mississippi! You can tell as soon as you cross it that you're in a different domain, a new realm. The Heartland—isn't that what you call it up here? The "Heartland"?

EMMA: Dairyland, actually. "America's Dairyland." It's on the license plates.

WELCH: I noticed that.

EMMA: But it's all moved away.

WELCH: What has?

EMMA: The milk. The cows.

WELCH: But you've got cows down there.

EMMA: There's just a few of us left.

WELCH: Who?

EMMA: Dairy—dairy people.

WELCH: Well, where'd they go? Where'd they move away to?

EMMA: Out west. Agribusiness. Big corporations.

WELCH: Fascinating.

EMMA: Look, if you'd like me to call my husband, I can just ring the bell and he'll come up.

(*She moves toward door.*)

WELCH: No! No need for that. I wouldn't want to take him away from his chores. Good to see a man carrying out simple, traditional farm chores these days, without complaint. Almost as a sense of duty. It would certainly cut down on our dependency for foreigners, wouldn't it?

EMMA: What?

WELCH: More men like your husband. Willing and able.

EMMA: What exactly do you want? What are you doing here?

WELCH: We're on a kind of a survey of sorts.

EMMA: We?

WELCH: Yes—a survey and a—search, let's say.

EMMA: Who's "we"?

WELCH: Well, I'm not really allowed to reveal my affiliations exactly. Let's just say we're on a kind of a talent search for solid citizens who own their own land outright. Are you sure you're not interested in a cookie?

EMMA: I'm positive.

WELCH: Plenty more in my attaché case.

EMMA: No.

WELCH: Suit yourself. We've targeted certain outlying areas we feel might have potential—

EMMA: Targeted?

WELCH: Yes, that's right. This house, for instance—

EMMA: What?

WELCH: Your house—the farm—

EMMA: It's not mine alone. It belongs to me and my husband. We're partners.

WELCH: Of course you are. That's well understood. How many rooms?

EMMA: What?

WELCH: In the house.

EMMA: Oh—five—with the den. I think.

WELCH: Five?

EMMA: Yes. Why?

WELCH: No basement?

EMMA: Well—yes.

WELCH: Then six. With the basement.

EMMA: Well, if you want to call the basement a room.

WELCH: What else would you call it?

EMMA: A basement.

WELCH: Yes. Well, let's just say six then.

EMMA: With the basement?

WELCH: That's right. Anyone down there?

EMMA: What?

WELCH: In the basement. Anyone down there now in the basement?

EMMA: No—why would there be?

WELCH: Well, it's not my house, Emma. How am I supposed to know who's down there in your basement or why they would be?

EMMA: There's nobody down in my basement and how do you know my name?

(WELCH *moves toward basement stairs.*)

WELCH: You're sure there's no one down there? Right now, as we speak?

EMMA: I would like you to leave, please! I would like you to get the heck out of my house! You're making me very nervous.

(WELCH *stops abruptly, turns to her, and smiles.*)

WELCH: Of course.

EMMA: Now!

(WELCH *goes quickly to counter, grabs his case, and heads for door.* EMMA *stops him.*)

Wait a second. Do you have a card or something? Some kind of identification? A name?

(WELCH *stops with his back to her.*)

WELCH: I couldn't help noticing your flagpole out front.

EMMA: What?

WELCH: Your flagpole.

EMMA: What about it?

WELCH: (*turning to her with a smile*) It's empty. Barren. Just the raw wind slapping the naked ropes around. Sickening sound.

EMMA: So what?

WELCH: Well, Emma, this is Wisconsin, isn't it? I'm not in Bulgaria or Turkistan or somewhere lost in the Balkans. I'm in Wisconsin. Taxidermy and cheese! Part of the U.S. of A. You told me that yourself.

EMMA: What are you driving at?

WELCH: You'd think there would be a flag up or something to that effect. Some sign. Some indication of loyalty and pride.

EMMA: Loyalty? To Wisconsin?

WELCH: (*pacing through room*) Nothing in here either. Not even one small token in the home. No miniature Mount Rushmore, Statue of Liberty, no weeping bald eagles clutching arrows. Nothing like that. We could be anywhere.

EMMA: We're not anywhere.

WELCH: Well, you and I know that, Emma, but what about the rest of the world? What about the people driving by—the Everyday Joes? Wouldn't they like to look up here and be reminded of their proud heritage?

EMMA: I don't know about the rest of the world.

WELCH: What's that dripping sound?

EMMA: What?

WELCH: That dripping.

EMMA: Oh, I just watered the plants. They're dripping.

WELCH: I see. You have some sort of empathy with plants, I suppose?

EMMA: I like them, yes. Especially through the winter.

WELCH: I imagine it can get pretty grim out here in January.

EMMA: You have no idea.

(WELCH *goes to couch, sets his case down on it, and pops it open.*)

WELCH: Well, there are many ways to brighten a place up, Emma—we have a wide variety of patriotic paraphernalia available.

EMMA: I wish you wouldn't call me by my name. It's very confusing.

WELCH: Why is that?

EMMA: Well, it feels as though I should know you, but I don't know you.

WELCH: You could know me.

EMMA: I don't.

WELCH: You could get to know me.

EMMA: I don't want to get to know you!

WELCH: Just take a look at what we have here, Emma.

(*He pulls out an accordion string of small American flags from his case and holds it up for* EMMA.)

A starter kit of your basic grassroots flag and decal ensemble. Five ninety-five for the full set of six. Then, from there, you can move right on up to the Proud Patriot package for twelve fifty, which includes banners, whistles, parade equipment, fireworks—complete with a brand-new remixed CD of Pat Boone singing the "Battle Hymn of the Republic."

EMMA: No! No, thank you!

WELCH: This also qualifies you for a forty percent discount on a brand-new red, white, and blue bullhorn in three unique sizes.

EMMA: No!! I am not in the market!

(*Pause.* WELCH *folds up the string of flags and puts it back in case.*)

WELCH: Not in the market. Not in the market. Well—you don't know how disappointed certain influential parties are going to be about this, Emma. You have no idea.

EMMA: Who are you, anyway? What is your name? What are you doing in my house?

WELCH: Your house—yes—did you say six rooms?

EMMA: What?

WELCH: Here in the house. Six rooms?

EMMA: Well—including the basement.

WELCH: Including the basement. That's right. And you're
   sure there's no one down there?

EMMA: Yes, I am—sure.

WELCH: Swear on a stack of bibles?

EMMA: I don't have to—

WELCH: Good-bye, Emma.

(*He snaps the case shut and abruptly exits front door.*)

EMMA: What? Wait a minute! Hey!

(*She watches* WELCH *cross past the window outside and disap-
pear off left. She runs out on the porch and rings the old school
bell for* FRANK. *She yells out to* FRANK *across the frozen fields.*)

Frank!! Frank! Come on up here, would ya, Frank!

(*She comes back into the house, pauses, and looks around,
slightly stunned, trying to figure out the whole encounter with*
WELCH. *She goes back out on porch and rings bell again.
Calls out to* FRANK.)

Frank!! Come on up here!

(*She stops ringing bell and waves vigorously for* FRANK *to come up to the house. She comes back into the house and crosses to the basement staircase. She yells down to their guest.*)

Mr. Haynes! Mr. Haynes, are you up yet? I'm making breakfast, if you're interested! Bacon. Crispy bacon.

(*No answer. She goes to stove and resumes frying up bacon. She calls out again from stove in a singsong voice.*)

Oh, Mr. Haynes!

(FRANK *appears outside on porch, stomping his feet to get the snow and mud off.* EMMA *jumps at the sound.* FRANK *enters.*)

FRANK: (*slightly winded from the hike*) Why'd you ring the bell?

(EMMA *turns and crosses to him. She looks out the windows.*)

EMMA: There was a man here. Did you see him?

FRANK: A man?

EMMA: Yeah. Did you see him?

FRANK: I was graining the heifers.

EMMA: A man came up here to the house. He was wearing a suit—briefcase. You didn't see him?

FRANK. I didn't see any man. Nope. You called me all the way up here to the house—

EMMA: He was just here. He must've gone right past you.

FRANK: What'd he want?

EMMA: He just showed up outa the blue. Just walked right in. I thought maybe you had an appointment with him or something.

FRANK: An appointment?

EMMA: Yeah.

FRANK: An appointment.

EMMA: That's what I said!

FRANK: When was the last time you can remember me having an appointment?

(FRANK *moves to couch, sits, and removes his boots, then tosses them out on mud porch. He wriggles his toes inside his socks to warm them up.*)

I could be down there graining my heifers.

EMMA: Well, what do you suppose he wanted?

FRANK: I didn't see any man.

EMMA: He knew my name.

FRANK: Well, what'd he say?

EMMA: Wanted to know how many rooms there were in the house.

FRANK: This house?

EMMA: Yes. This house—our house.

FRANK: Well, what'd you tell him?

EMMA: Five, I said. Then he corrected me.

FRANK: He corrected you?

EMMA: Yeah. He said there was six—including the basement.

FRANK: Well, that's true enough, I guess. If you call the basement a room.

EMMA: Now you're taking his side.

FRANK: I don't even know this guy.

(FRANK *gets up and crosses to stove in his stocking feet, moves the bacon around with fork.*)

EMMA: Why would he care about the house? How many rooms there are.

FRANK: You got me.

EMMA: Maybe he wants to buy it.

FRANK: This bacon looks burnt.

EMMA: You didn't see him go by on your way back up?

FRANK: Nope.

EMMA: I don't see how you could have missed him. You didn't see any car?

FRANK: Yeah, I saw a car.

EMMA: You did?

FRANK: (*forking bacon*) Yeah—I saw a couple cars.

EMMA: Two?

FRANK: Is Graig up yet?

EMMA: No—no, I don't think so. I yelled down to him but—

(FRANK *crosses to top of basement stairs and yells down.*)

FRANK: Graig! Graig, get your sorry ass up here if you want some breakfast! This isn't a boardinghouse! Rise and shine!

(FRANK *returns to stove and bacon.*)

How'd you manage to burn this bacon, anyway?

EMMA: Frank—there were two cars?

FRANK: What?

EMMA: Two cars out there?

FRANK: I don't know, Emma. Two or three. What difference does it make?

EMMA: Three?

FRANK: I wasn't counting!

EMMA: Where were they?

FRANK: On the road.

EMMA: Out front?

FRANK: Yes! On the road, out front. What's the matter with you? That's what cars do. They go up and down on the road, out front. Where else would they go?

EMMA: Well, so they could've just been plain old ordinary everyday cars then, couldn't they? Just passersby.

FRANK: As opposed to what?

EMMA: Government cars.

FRANK: Government cars?

EMMA: Dark cars. Suspicious. Tinted windows. Unmarked Chevys. Black antennas bowed over. That kind of thing.

FRANK: Where do you get this stuff?

EMMA: I know, Frank. I'm not uninformed. I know about this stuff.

FRANK: I was feeding my heifers. I didn't notice what cars they were or if their antennas were bowed over.

EMMA: Did you catch their license plates?

FRANK: When I'm feeding the heifers, time stands still for me. Nothing else exists.

(HAYNES, *their guest, is suddenly standing at the top of the basement stair landing in a plaid bathrobe, rubbing the morning crust out of his eyes.*)

HAYNES: Morning—

(EMMA *jumps slightly, turns toward him.*)

FRANK: Get enough sleep?

HAYNES: Was somebody ringing a bell up here?

(EMMA *crosses to* HAYNES, *enthusiastically.*)

EMMA: Oh, yes, that was me. We have a bell—Frank's told me so much about you. I was asleep when you came in last night. I'm so sorry I didn't stay up to meet you.

HAYNES: Oh, that's all right.

EMMA: I'm Emma—

(*As* EMMA *gets closer to* HAYNES, *he backs up slightly, holding his hand out timidly, and as soon as* EMMA *touches his hand to shake it, a bright blue flash of light emanates from* HAYNES*'s fingers.* EMMA *screams and jumps back.* HAYNES *shakes his hand violently as though it were severely burned.*)

What was that! (*to* FRANK) Did you see that? What the heck was that?

HAYNES: Static shock. I'm sorry. I apologize. I never know quite how to explain this.

EMMA: Static shock?

HAYNES: Yes. That's what it is. It gets worse and worse each year. Especially in the winter. Maybe it's the ozone or something.

EMMA: Ozone?

HAYNES: I don't know. I'm very sorry.

EMMA: Oh, you don't have to apologize. You can't help it, I guess. I'm assuming—

HAYNES: No, it's true—I can't.

EMMA: I've just never seen anything quite like that. I mean, I've had static shock before, but—rugs and doorknobs and stuff, but—

FRANK: Yeah, that's pretty impressive, Graig. You pick that up out there in Colorado or something?

(FRANK *crosses to couch, chewing bacon and carrying coffee.*)

EMMA: Would you like some bacon, Mr. Haynes? And coffee—there's coffee too. Help yourself.

HAYNES: Thanks.

(EMMA *crosses to stove.* FRANK *sits on couch with bacon and coffee.* FRANK *sings a short snatch from an old song.*)

FRANK: (*singing*) "My baby loves bacon
          And that's what I'm makin'
          When I'm cookin' breakfast for the one
          I love.
          I don't like oatmeal . . ."

EMMA: Oh, don't sing that, Frank. We've got company. (*to* HAYNES) He always sings that when we have company.

FRANK: We never have company.

EMMA: That's not entirely true.

(HAYNES *shivers, rubs his arms.*)

HAYNES: How cold is it out there, anyway?

EMMA: Oh, it's plenty cold.

FRANK: Cold enough to stick your tongue to a mailbox.

EMMA: How cold was it back there in Colorado, Mr. Haynes?

HAYNES: Graig.

EMMA: What?

HAYNES: Call me Graig.

EMMA: Craig? Oh—all right—Craig.

HAYNES: No, Graig—with a G.

EMMA: What?

HAYNES: Never mind.

EMMA: Would you like a cup of coffee, Craig?

HAYNES: Please—yes.

(*She pours him a cup.*)

EMMA: So, how cold was it back there in Colorado, Craig?

(FRANK *stands suddenly from the couch, throwing down his coffee cup. Violent.*)

FRANK: GRAIG! His name is Graig! Didn't you hear him? Graig with a G, not Craig with a C! GRAIG!!

EMMA: (*flatly*) Oh, my God.

(EMMA *slams down coffeepot and exits out through kitchen archway, stage left. Pause.* FRANK *picks up his cup off the floor and takes it to the sink. Pause.*)

HAYNES: I didn't mean to upset her.

FRANK: You didn't.

HAYNES: She seemed upset.

FRANK: She was, but you weren't the cause of it.

HAYNES: Oh—

FRANK: Some man came by, evidently—some stranger. I guess that's it. Got her shook up.

HAYNES: A stranger?

FRANK: That's what she said. She gets nervous. We hardly ever see anyone out here.

HAYNES: Well—what did he want?

FRANK: Who?

HAYNES: The stranger.

FRANK: You got me. I didn't see him. I was down feeding my heifers.

HAYNES: She didn't say?

FRANK: Not really. Just asked her a bunch of strange questions about the house.

HAYNES: What kind of questions?

FRANK: Nothing, really. I mean—how many rooms there were. Stuff like that.

HAYNES: That's strange, isn't it?

FRANK: What?

HAYNES: A stranger coming by.

FRANK: Not really. We're out here in the boondocks. Sitting ducks for solicitors.

HAYNES: Oh, really?

FRANK: Yeah, sure. All kinds. They see the house from the road, all exposed like this. They come up. We're vulnerable.

HAYNES: Do you mind if I have a piece of bacon? It smells so good.

FRANK: It's burnt.

HAYNES: I don't mind. I like it crispy.

FRANK: Help yourself.

(HAYNES *goes to stove, takes bacon, sips coffee.*)

HAYNES: Well, what are they soliciting, these solicitors?

FRANK: Protein lick, calf booster, ivermectin, steroid tags, lactose, dehorners, lice powder—you name it.

HAYNES: Never occurred to me there'd be salesmen out here.

FRANK: Why not? There's salesmen everywhere. Every time you turn around there's another salesman. Whole country's made of salesmen.

HAYNES: Yeah, I guess.

(HAYNES *crosses to windows with coffee and bacon, stands in front of plants, looking out.*)

Well, I just hope I'm not intruding here. I mean, I didn't mean to cause any tension.

FRANK: There's no tension. What makes you think that?

HAYNES: I don't know—

FRANK: There's no tension here. We're in the country here. Everything's quiet and peaceful.

HAYNES: Well, I just really appreciate you and your wife letting me stay here, Frank.

FRANK: You'd do the same for me.

HAYNES: I would. You bet. The situation back there just got—very complicated.

FRANK: Situation?

HAYNES: Yeah. You know—

FRANK: Oh, you mean back there in Rocky Buttes or whatever you call it.

(HAYNES *wheels around suddenly to* FRANK. *Just stares at him.*)

What?

HAYNES: Where'd you hear that name?

FRANK: What, Rocky Buttes?

HAYNES: Don't say that name!

FRANK: That's what you told me on the phone.

HAYNES: I never told you that. That's not something I would have told you. It's top secret! Does she know?

FRANK: Who?

HAYNES: Your wife! Emma. Does she know?

FRANK: What?

HAYNES: The name!

FRANK: Rocky Buttes?

(HAYNES *leaps toward* FRANK, *grabbing him by the shoulders and covering his mouth.*)

HAYNES: Stop saying that name! I told you not to say it! What's the matter with you? That was one of the first things I told you on the phone. That was one of our contingencies. Wasn't it?

(FRANK *can't answer with* HAYNES's *hand over his mouth.*)

Wasn't it?!

(HAYNES *releases him. Pause.* FRANK *wipes his mouth.*)

FRANK: You better settle down, Graig.

HAYNES: I'm sorry.

FRANK: We lead a very peaceful life here. We're in the country. We're dairy farmers.

HAYNES: I'm sorry. I just can't take any chances. Maybe, after this thing blows over—

FRANK: What thing?

HAYNES: This whole—crisis.

FRANK: Are we talking about a world situation or something personal, Graig?

HAYNES: What's the difference?

(*Pause.* HAYNES *rubs his arms from the cold. He moves to windows and looks out over the fields below.*)

God, it's cold.

FRANK: Yeah. You'll get used to it.

HAYNES: Are those your cows down there below?

FRANK: They're not cows. They're replacement heifers.

HAYNES: Oh—

FRANK: Those are my babies.

HAYNES: What are they replacing?

FRANK: Older cows. Retired cows.

HAYNES: Oh, I see. Yeah, I remember.

FRANK: They haven't had a calf yet. Every year you save some back.

HAYNES: Unbred?

FRANK: Exactly. The mama cows are up in the top pasture.

HAYNES: So you're going to breed them then, is that it? These replacement heifers?

FRANK: I plan to. Yes.

HAYNES: You've got the bull?

FRANK: He's out back.

HAYNES: What are you waiting for?

FRANK: Spring.

(*Pause.* HAYNES *keeps staring out window.*)

HAYNES: Do you know what plutonium is named after, Frank?

FRANK: What? Plutonium?

HAYNES: Yes.

FRANK: No—what?

HAYNES: Pluto—the god of hell.

FRANK: Oh—I thought he was a cartoon.

HAYNES: Do you know how long it remains radioactive and biologically dangerous once it's released into the atmosphere?

FRANK: Plutonium?

HAYNES: Yes.

FRANK: No, I don't know anything about it.

HAYNES: Five hundred thousand years.

FRANK: That's a long time.

HAYNES: It is. The most carcinogenic substance known to man. It causes mutations in the genes of the reproductive cells. The eggs and the sperm. Major mutations. A kind of random compulsory genetic engineering that goes on and on and on and on.

FRANK: That would probably affect my heifers then, wouldn't it?

HAYNES: Yes, it would, Frank. It definitely would affect your heifers. It would affect every heifer within six hundred miles of here. It would penetrate the food chain and bio-accumulate thousands of times over, lasting generation after generation. Tasteless, odorless, and invisible.

FRANK: Is that what this is all about, Graig? Is that why you had to come out here? This random, compulsory genetic thing?

(*Long pause.* HAYNES *stares out window.*)

HAYNES: Looks like your man is back.

FRANK: What?

HAYNES: Your stranger. Is that him down there?

FRANK: I never saw him. What's he doing?

(FRANK *moves fast to window, looks out.*)

HAYNES: That's probably him.

FRANK: What's he doing down there?

HAYNES: Looks like he's walking around with your heifers.

FRANK: In the pen? He's in the pen with my heifers?

HAYNES: Looks like. Isn't he right inside there with them?

FRANK: I'll be right back.

HAYNES: Be careful, Frank. You don't know this guy.

(FRANK *rushes out on porch, grabs his coat, and exits.* HAYNES *watches him cross window outside.* EMMA *appears in half-light of archway by kitchen. She just stands there staring at* HAYNES. HAYNES *turns toward her. Pause.*)

What's that dripping sound?

EMMA: The plants. I overwater them. I can't help myself.

(HAYNES *smiles. He reaches out and touches one of* EMMA's *plants. Again, the brilliantly bright flash of blue light comes from his hand.* HAYNES *jumps back. Black out.*)

Scene Two

Same set: Next morning. EMMA *going through same routine—watering plants, back and forth to the sink with the pitcher.* HAYNES *sits on couch with his back partially to audience, sipping coffee, watching* EMMA. *Pause for a while as* EMMA *just waters and* HAYNES *just sips.*

EMMA: (*continuing to water*) You're up bright and early.

HAYNES: Yes—where's Frank?

EMMA: Feeding the heifers. He's always feeding the heifers.

HAYNES: He seems very devoted to them.

EMMA: He is. It's his life's work.

HAYNES: I'm glad to see he's finally found something.

EMMA: Yes. You two must have gone very different ways.

HAYNES: How do you mean?

EMMA: Well, I mean—your work—your research.

HAYNES: My research?

EMMA: Yes. Whatever it is—I don't know. It's different.

HAYNES: Different than what?

EMMA: Frank. Different than what Frank chose.

HAYNES: Oh, yes. Sure. I see.

EMMA: I mean Frank never had any aspirations like that. He's always been very content in the country. Farming. Animal husbandry, hybrid vigor. Stuff like that.

HAYNES: Sure. I see what you mean. Hybrid vigor?

EMMA: Whereas, you—you're off working for the government, doing important research.

HAYNES: I'm not in research. I'm not doing any research.

EMMA: Oh—well, Frank told me—

HAYNES: Frank was mistaken.

EMMA: Oh. He told me he thought you were working for the government.

HAYNES: No. I'm not.

EMMA: Out there somewhere in a place called Rocky Buttes or something.

(HAYNES *stands abruptly, knocking over the coffee.*)

HAYNES: Oh—I'm sorry. I'm just—

EMMA: Don't worry about it.

(*She hurries to sink, gets a sponge, comes back, and cleans up mess.* HAYNES *just stands there.*)

HAYNES: I'm so sorry. I've been kind of shaky lately.

EMMA: It's all right. It's probably all that static shock.

HAYNES: Well, no—it's not that so much. It's just a whole accumulation of things.

EMMA: (*cleaning up*) Well, don't worry.

HAYNES: Things piling up.

EMMA: I understand.

HAYNES: That's why I thought it would be good to get away for a while. Come out here and—just get away.

EMMA: Sure.

HAYNES: I hope you don't mind. I mean—

EMMA: It's fine. Really. Wisconsin is the perfect getaway. Nothing ever happens here. People have been coming here for a hundred years because nothing ever happens. Every once in a while someone falls through the ice or gets beheaded on their snowmobile, but other than that—

HAYNES: Beheaded?

EMMA: On their snowmobile. You know—going so darn fast they don't see the barbed-wire fence and— (*draws a line across her neck*)

HAYNES: Oh—I'm very sorry about the spill. Is it going to ruin the sofa?

EMMA: Oh, don't worry about that. It's beyond ruin. It's seen way worse than coffee spills. Premature calves. Afterbirth. Blood all over the place. You can't wreck it. More coffee?

HAYNES: Yes—well, no—well, yes, I guess I will. Yes.

EMMA: That's a yes?

HAYNES: Yes. Thanks.

EMMA: Good.

(*She gets him another cup of coffee. Pause.*)

HAYNES: How long have you lived out here? You and Frank?

EMMA: Well, I've lived here all my life.

HAYNES: Oh—a native? I didn't know that.

EMMA: Yes. I was born in this house, as a matter of fact. Right in this room. Right on the spot you're standing, actually.

HAYNES: Oh—

(*He looks down at floor and quickly jumps away from spot he's standing on.*)

EMMA: That's all right. It's not sacred or anything.

HAYNES: That's amazing. I don't think I've ever met anyone like that.

EMMA: Like what?

HAYNES: Well, you know—born and raised in the same house, still living in the same place. Same spot—

EMMA: There's a few of us left.

(*She returns to watering.*)

HAYNES: That's amazing.

EMMA: It's funny what different people find amazing.

HAYNES: Aren't you afraid of drowning those plants?

EMMA: I'm not afraid of anything.

HAYNES: (*short pause*) No, but I mean—some plants don't like to be sitting in water all the time. The roots—

EMMA: It's the winters.

HAYNES: Sorry?

EMMA: The winters, out here.

HAYNES: Oh—

EMMA: They cause behavior like this. You have no idea. You get into these habits. These trains of thought. If I—if I didn't water like this, I wouldn't know what to

do with myself. There would be a horrible gap. I might
fall in.

HAYNES: I see.

EMMA: I suppose you never have this problem in your line
of work. Everything must be so exciting all the time.
Out there in the West—

HAYNES: Well, not really.

EMMA: No? All that danger? The uncertainty?

HAYNES: Danger?

EMMA: Yes. The torture! I mean, I couldn't believe that
part of it.

HAYNES: Torture? Look—I don't know what Frank's been
telling you, but—

EMMA: Oh, I know it's all top secret and you're not
allowed to talk about it.

HAYNES: Talk about what?

EMMA: Rocky Buttes—all that stuff.

(HAYNES *stands again very abruptly, upset.*)

HAYNES: Stop saying that over and over again! Like it's some kind of code or something!

EMMA: I'm sorry. I didn't realize—

HAYNES: Frank wasn't even supposed to mention it!

EMMA: I'm very sorry.

HAYNES: I wouldn't even have come out here if I'd known he was going to blab it all over the place!

EMMA: Blab? He didn't blab. Frank's not a blabber.

HAYNES: He blabbed to you!

EMMA: I'm his wife!

HAYNES: It's still blabbing! A breach of trust!

(HAYNES *suddenly gets ahold of himself and stops. Pause.* EMMA *somewhat shocked by the outburst.*)

I'm—sorry.

EMMA: You must be under a great deal of stress, Mr. Haynes.

HAYNES: Yes. I'm very sorry. I—I should just go back down in the basement.

EMMA: There's no need for that.

HAYNES: I don't mean to—something's—happening to me.

EMMA: What is it? Would you like me to—

HAYNES: No!

EMMA: I could call a doctor.

HAYNES: No, I'm fine!

EMMA: Those blue flashes—that's not normal, Mr. Haynes. I mean, I've had static shock before—

HAYNES: That's what it is! Static shock! Severe static shock! Why don't you believe me?

EMMA: I do believe you.

HAYNES: No, you don't! You just told me it wasn't normal.

EMMA: Well, it's not normal to have lightning flashes coming out of your body, is it?

HAYNES: It's not lightning, it's static shock!!

EMMA: All right, all right! Golly.

(*Pause.*)

HAYNES: I'll just go back down in the basement until Frank comes up. I never should have left the basement in the first place.

(HAYNES *heads for basement.* EMMA *stops him.*)

EMMA: No, please. Don't go back down in the basement. There's no windows down there. No air. I feel like such a bad hostess.

HAYNES: No, not at all. It's not you, it's me. I just need to be alone for a while. Please—

(HAYNES *tries to go past* EMMA *to get to the basement. She grabs his elbow, trying to stop him, and another bright blue flash comes from* HAYNES. EMMA *steps back quickly.*)

Don't keep touching me!

EMMA: I'm sorry. I just—I'm very sorry. Jeepers.

HAYNES: I never should have come here!

EMMA: No, please—please—it's so nice to have some company for a change. We never see anyone out here. Me and Frank. The mailman now and then. The propane delivery truck. The driver. They wave to us from the road. We wave back. But we never talk to anyone.

HAYNES: Don't you have some neighbors?

EMMA: They never come out. It's too cold.

HAYNES: How 'bout summer?

EMMA: Summer they stay in the air-conditioning.

HAYNES: Don't they farm too?

EMMA: Nobody farms anymore. Government pays them not to. We're the only ones left.

HAYNES: How come you and Frank do it?

EMMA: Frank loves his heifers.

HAYNES: Oh—

EMMA: He lives for his heifers.

HAYNES: I see—

EMMA: Don't you want more coffee?

HAYNES: Well—

EMMA: Please—

HAYNES: All right.

(*She gets him more coffee. Pause.*)

Did a man come by here yesterday? Frank said something about a man. A stranger.

EMMA: Yes. Weirdest thing. He just walked right in here like he owned the place.

HAYNES: What did he want?

EMMA: I'm not sure. At first he was trying to force a cookie on me.

HAYNES: A cookie?

EMMA: Yes. An American flag cookie.

HAYNES: Did you accept?

EMMA: What?

HAYNES: The cookie.

EMMA: No. Of course not.

HAYNES: What else did he want?

EMMA: Wanted to know how many rooms there were in the house and who was living in the basement.

HAYNES: The basement?

EMMA: Yes.

HAYNES: He asked you that?

EMMA: Yes.

HAYNES: The basement, specifically?

EMMA: Yes, he did.

HAYNES: Well, nobody's living in the basement.

EMMA: That's what I told him.

HAYNES: You did?

EMMA: Yes, I did.

HAYNES: And that's not a lie, is it? Because I'm technically not "living" in the basement—I'm just staying down there for a little while—just visiting. I'm your guest, in fact.

EMMA: Yes, that's right. You are.

HAYNES: You didn't tell him that, did you?

EMMA: What?

HAYNES: That you had a guest down there—living in the basement?

EMMA: No—no, of course not. You're not "living" down there, anyway. There's no hot plate, no bathroom.

HAYNES: No, I mean, you didn't even mention me, did you?

EMMA: No.

HAYNES: Good.

EMMA: I didn't.

HAYNES: That's good. And did he seem to buy that or did he seem to think you were lying?

EMMA: Well, I wasn't lying.

HAYNES: No, I know that. You and I both know that, but what about him? Did he seem to accept what you were saying at face value? That you were telling the truth?

EMMA: He didn't seem the least bit interested in that.

HAYNES: In what?

EMMA: The truth.

(*Suddenly, the doorbell rings. Very loud this time. They both jump and stare at the door. Pause.*)

HAYNES: (*heavy whisper*) That's him!

EMMA: (*whisper*) Who?

HAYNES: (*whisper*) Him. Don't answer it.

EMMA: (*whispers back*) How do you know?

HAYNES: (*whisper*) This is the way they operate. They're relentless.

(*Doorbell rings again.* HAYNES *bolts for the basement staircase.* EMMA *stops him by running in front of him without touching him.*)

EMMA: Who are they?

HAYNES: Just don't let him in. Whatever you do, don't let him in!

EMMA: Please, don't go down in the basement, Mr. Haynes.

HAYNES: You don't know me. You've never seen me. I don't exist.

(*Doorbell rings again. Even louder.* HAYNES *bolts down staircase and disappears.* EMMA *alone.*)

EMMA: Oh, criminy! Jeepers!

(*She crosses over to door, stops, but doesn't open it. She yells through door.*)

Who is it?

WELCH'S VOICE: It's me again, Emma! It's only me.

(EMMA *backs away at sound of his voice.*)

EMMA: Who?

WELCH'S VOICE: You know who, Emma. I came by yesterday with the cookies. Remember?

EMMA: What do you want this time? And how in the heck do you know my name?

WELCH'S VOICE: I'd just like to ask you some more questions about the house.

EMMA: No! No more questions! You just get away from here. Go down and see my husband. He's down there by the barn. You go down there and ask him your questions. Don't ask me.

WELCH'S VOICE: I've already seen your husband, Emma.

EMMA: You have?

WELCH'S VOICE: Yes, I saw him yesterday.

EMMA: He told me he never saw you.

WELCH'S VOICE: Well, I had a good long talk with him.

EMMA: And what did he say?

WELCH'S VOICE: He said he thought we could work something out.

(WELCH *opens door and steps right in, closing door behind him.* EMMA *backs up.*)

EMMA: Don't! Don't you dare come in here! What're you doing!?

WELCH: He said you wouldn't mind.

EMMA: Well, I do mind! You can't just come busting into people's houses like this. Who do you think you are?

WELCH: Busting? I wouldn't exactly call this busting. The door was open—

EMMA: The door was open because this is Wisconsin and we all leave our doors open in Wisconsin! It's the open-door policy.

WELCH: Well, that's a charming custom.

EMMA: It's not a custom, it's a trust. Now, get out!

(WELCH *smiles and heads toward basement stairs.*)

EMMA: Where are you going now?

WELCH: This issue about the basement still bothers me.

EMMA: What issue? There's no issue. Stay away from my basement!

WELCH: Whether or not it can officially be called a room.

EMMA: Officially?

WELCH: I suppose, technically speaking, it could only be called a room if someone were actually living down there. Isn't that right? A room is where someone lives. Otherwise it's just a space. An empty space.

EMMA: There's no one living down there. I told you that.

WELCH: I know you told me that, Emma, but we have other information.

EMMA: What information? Who's "we"?

WELCH: Highly classified information. Now, I suppose we could resort to high-priority tactics if we were forced to, but I'd rather not go down that road if we can possibly avoid it.

EMMA: What kind of tactics are those?

WELCH: Flushing tactics.

EMMA: Flushing?

WELCH: For flushing out fugitives.

EMMA: He's not a fugitive!

WELCH: Aah! So there is someone living down there, isn't there, Emma?

EMMA: No!

WELCII: No?

EMMA: He's not a fugitive. He's a friend of my husband's. And he's not even down there anymore. He was here for a day and then he left.

WELCH: Where did he go?

EMMA: I have no idea.

WELCH: Just vanished.

EMMA: Yup.

WELCH: Just—walked off into the night. Poof!

EMMA: Guess so.

WELCH: Why don't you go down there now and bring him up for me, Emma? Be a good girl.

EMMA: There's no one down there!

WELCH: You know, we are very, very skilled at flushing rats out of their nests. We've had vast experience. You wouldn't want to see a bunker buster come blasting into your little kitchen from heaven knows where, would you? Because we can arrange that, Emma. It's just a phone call away.

EMMA: What's he done? He's not a criminal, is he?

WELCH: He hasn't done a thing, Emma. Not a thing. We'd just like to speak to him. Now, I can go down there myself or you could help things along by coaxing him up here for me.

EMMA: (*yelling downstairs*) Mr. Haynes! Mr. Haynes, are you down there? (*pause, no answer*) See? Nobody down there. Not a soul.

WELCH: (*smiles*) Haynes? Is that what he's calling himself now? Interesting.

EMMA: There's nobody down there!

WELCH: (*loudly, so* HAYNES *can hear*) Well, I suppose we'll just have to order up some smoke!

EMMA: Smoke?

WELCH: Some gas, maybe.

EMMA: Gas? You're not bringing smoke and gas into my home! My plants can't take it.

WELCH: Well, we could flood him out, I suppose. Takes a little longer, but just as effective. There's always fire, but then we'd be losing the house, wouldn't we?

EMMA: I'm going down to get my husband!

(EMMA *heads for the door.*)

WELCH: Good idea! You do that. Maybe he could help us out with this pesky Mr. Haynes.

EMMA: (*turning to* WELCH) Don't you underestimate my husband, mister! Frank can be a very ill-tempered man if he wants to. It doesn't take much to set him off.

WELCH: I'm sure you're right about that.

EMMA: You better be gone when he gets back here. I'm telling you, he's got a very short fuse. Last year we had some deer hunters break through our bottom pasture, and you should have seen Frank. He went absolutely berserk. Chased them off with a twelve-gauge.

(WELCH *just smiles and chuckles at her.* EMMA *runs out onto porch and rings the school bell again. She calls out to* FRANK.)

(*outside*) Frank!! Frank!!! Get up here, would you!!

(EMMA *runs off porch, yelling for* FRANK, *and exits. Pause.* WELCH, *alone, talks down the staircase to an unseen* HAYNES.)

WELCH: Well, well, well—Mr. "Haynes," is that it? Mr. Haynes? Very inventive. Deceptively simple. Almost poetic. "Haynes"—rhymes with "pains," or is it "shames"? Possibly. Could even be "blames." The choices are endless. Well, not exactly endless. Everything has its limits, I suppose. Everything runs into a brick wall sooner or later. Even the most heroic ideas.

(WELCH *crosses to kitchen counter, sets his attaché case down on it, and pops the case open.*)

Sooner or later it would come down to just a finite number of possibilities, wouldn't it, Haynes? Brains, maims, flames, chains. Which is it? What's it going to be?

(HAYNES *appears at top of stairs, head slumped down, shoulders slouched.* WELCH *smiles at him, then pulls out the long string of tiny American flags from his case along with a large chrome staple gun. He climbs up on kitchen counter with the string of flags and stapler, continuing to talk to* HAYNES. *He starts stapling the string of flags to the cupboards above the sink.*)

There he is! There he finally is. Looking just a wee bit sheepish and downtrodden. We've been hunting all over for you, buddy-boy. You've caused us a great deal of anxiety. Not to mention the exorbitant and unnecessary expense.

HAYNES: How did you track me down?

(*Everything is now being punctuated by the shots from the staple gun.*)

WELCH: You left a very luminous trail, Mr. Haynes. Technology's a marvelous thing, though. Night vision. Infra-ray. It's extraordinary how blind the naked eye is. No wonder people have so much trouble accepting the truth these days.

HAYNES: I'm not going back, you know.

WELCH: Let's not start off on the wrong foot, buddy-boy.

HAYNES: I'm not going back!

WELCH: (*chuckles*) I'm afraid you're going to have to now. You're contaminated. You're a carrier. What're we going to do about that? We can't have you free-ranging all over the American countryside like some kind of headless chicken, can we? You've already endangered the lives of your friends here, not to mention the Midwest at large. Now, that was pretty selfish of you, wasn't it? Poisoning the Heartland?

HAYNES: You can't take me back there.

WELCH: Oh, come on now, "Haynes"—you were getting along so well. You can't just walk out in the middle of a project like that. You don't want to be known as a quitter, do you? Besides, we have a brand-new mission for you. Something of extreme international urgency. I'm sure you're going to want to be a part of it.

HAYNES: I'm not going back there! The whole state's going to explode. Colorado is going to be blown off the map.

WELCH: Why do you people have this incredible propensity for wild exaggeration? There's some minor leakage—we've acknowledged that. That's why you were hired in the first place, if you recall.

HAYNES: Minor leakage!

WELCH: That's all it was. The concrete wasn't thick enough.

HAYNES: The ground caught fire for thirty days! Not trees, not brush, but the raw earth!

WELCH: Fires have a way of burning themselves out, buddy-boy. It's nature's Band-Aid. Been going on for centuries. Chronicled. Spontaneous combustion. The Romans had it.

HAYNES: This wasn't lightning! This wasn't some renegade Boy Scout campfire like you ordered the press to print!

WELCH: It cleans things up, Haynes. Everything springs back to life in due time. We're doing nature a favor, as a matter of fact. We're provoking rebirth!

HAYNES: You can't just walk in here and take over. What are you doing to their house, anyway?

WELCH: Just a little decorating for our think tank. We have a big meeting coming up on Tuesday.

HAYNES: Where? Here?

WELCH: Exactly.

(*Throughout all this,* WELCH *keeps returning to his attaché case, pulling out more strings of American flags and stapling them up all over the house like some mad interior decorator.*)

HAYNES: No—look—you can't just co-opt their house. These are friends of mine.

WELCH: (*continues stapling*) We can do whatever we want, buddy-boy. That should be clear by now. We're in the driver's seat. Haven't you noticed? There's no more of that nonsense of checks and balances. All that red tape. All that hanging around in limbo, waiting for decisions from committees and tired-out lobbies. We're in absolute command now. We don't have to answer to a soul, least of all a couple of Wisconsin dairy farmers.

(HAYNES *crosses toward windows and porch. He looks out to pastures below.* WELCH *continues to staple the string of flags.*)

HAYNES: I never should have come here.

WELCH: We would have found you no matter what.

HAYNES: What have you done with them? Where'd they go?

WELCH: (*laughs*) Don't be such an alarmist.

HAYNES: Where did they go!?

WELCH: They're probably having a little powwow down at the barn. Talking things over.

HAYNES: What things?

WELCH: The future, Haynes! The bright, golden American future. You can just imagine what an enormous leap that is for a simple country couple like this—so out of touch. Living completely in the long ago. Stuck in some quaint pioneer morality.

HAYNES: (*crossing back toward* WELCH) They were just doing me a favor by letting me stay here. They're completely innocent!

WELCH: We're not interested in punishing them, Haynes. On the contrary, we're offering them a leg up. You, however, might be a serious candidate for punitive action.

HAYNES: I don't care what you do to me.

WELCH: No heroics, please.

HAYNES: I don't!

WELCH: No?

HAYNES: No.

WELCH: There's no memory anymore. That's the problem. No memory at all. Pearl Harbor. The Alamo. The Bataan Death March. All gone. Vanished like they never even happened. You don't want to start all over again, do you, Haynes?

HAYNES: All over where?

WELCH: You see? You don't remember a thing. That's exactly my point!

HAYNES: Remember what?

WELCH: The long, tedious procedure. The intensive training. The endless sleepless nights.

HAYNES: That was a long time ago!

WELCH: Yes! Now it begins to come back.

HAYNES: No!

WELCH: No?

HAYNES: I was younger then.

WELCH: Yes! Exactly. What would happen to your body now if you had to undergo the same ordeal? The same stress to your appendages.

HAYNES: I could take it!

WELCH: You could take it?

HAYNES: Yes, I could!

WELCH: The pain to your penis, for instance?

HAYNES: No!!! No!!

(HAYNES *suddenly grabs his crotch with both hands and holds on. A bolt of blue light shoots from his crotch.* HAYNES *just stands there, frozen, holding on to his crotch and staring out toward audience.* WELCH *stops stapling for a while, smiles at* HAYNES.)

WELCH: Some things do come back, don't they, Haynes? Some things do manage to penetrate all the false heroics, all the flimsy ideology. We're suddenly stung by our duty to a higher purpose. Our natural loyalties fall in line and we're amazed how simple it is to honor our one true heritage. Don't you find that to be the case now, Haynes?

(HAYNES, *still frozen, clutching his crotch, makes a muffled whining sound of acknowledgment.*)

We even know what the next step is, don't we, Haynes?

(HAYNES *nods vigorously.*)

The debriefing. The recoding. We know all that, don't we? We have it tucked away in our tiny dime-sized minds somewhere.

(HAYNES *nods again, still holding his crotch.*)

So, there's really nothing left for you to do but to go back down in the basement and wait for our team to come. Isn't that right, Haynes? Isn't that what you need to do now?

HAYNES: (*looking out at audience*) Do I really have to start all over?

WELCH: I don't know of any shortcuts. Do you, Haynes?

HAYNES: Can I still get my Krispy Kremes?

WELCH: Of course you can. You know you can. We would never deny you your Krispy Kremes.

(HAYNES, *still holding on to his crotch with both hands, starts moving slowly toward basement stairs.*)

HAYNES: My Mallomars?

WELCH: You bet.

HAYNES: My comic books?

WELCH: They're waiting for you back at Rocky Buttes.

(HAYNES *twitches at the sound of the name, and another blue flash comes from his crotch.*)

We'll have to get that twitching and flashing taken care of, though, Haynes. You can't walk around like a popping neon sign. We'll get that corrected for you back at base.

HAYNES: (*getting closer to stairs*) Do you think I could—I could have my music too? Do you remember my music?

WELCH: Well—I don't know about that. It might be possible. I'll try to pull some strings.

HAYNES: I'd like to hear my music again.

(HAYNES *goes down staircase and disappears.*)

WELCH: I'll do everything in my power, Haynes. Everything humanly possible.

(WELCH *resumes his stapling. Lights fade to black with sound of stapler as music comes in over the top and plays through break.*)

End Scene Two: MUSIC INTERLUDE

Scene Three

Same Set: Evening. EMMA *standing on kitchen counter taking down* WELCH's *string of flags.* FRANK *enters from outside through porch door dressed in suit and tie exactly like* WELCH's *and carrying an attaché case exactly like* WELCH's. *He walks very bowlegged and sore as though something terrible has happened to his genitalia. He hobbles to center of room, stops, and just stands there staring at* EMMA.

EMMA: (*standing on counter*) Where've you been? I was looking all over the place for you. Didn't you hear me? I was yelling and yelling—

FRANK: I didn't hear you.

(EMMA *climbs down from counter, bundling up string of flags in her arms, and crosses to* FRANK.)

EMMA: What's happened to you? What's the matter?

FRANK: I've sold the heifers.

EMMA: What?

FRANK: I sold the heifers. Money's in here. (*holds up case*)

EMMA: Why'd you do that, Frank? Those were your replacement heifers.

FRANK: Got a good price.

EMMA: What're you doing in that ridiculous suit?

FRANK: Mr. Welch gave it to me.

EMMA: Mr. Welch?

FRANK: Yes.

EMMA: That stranger? The one who barged in here asking about the house? Stringing up flags on my cupboards?

FRANK: That's the one. He bought my heifers too.

EMMA: No! Frank, you take that money back! You take it back right now. That's nuts—

FRANK: He's gone.

EMMA: Well, you go find him and give that money back! You've got no business—

FRANK: He won't be back here until Tuesday. There's going to be a meeting.

EMMA: A meeting? Where? Here? Not here there isn't

FRANK: That's what he said.

EMMA: This has gone far enough! I'm getting the sheriff out here.

FRANK: We don't need the sheriff. There's no crime. What's the crime?

EMMA: This guy is taking over our house! He's taking over our whole life! Stringing up flags! Forcing cookies on me! Who is this guy? We don't know him from Adam!

FRANK: He's from the government, Emma.

EMMA: Oh, you talked to him? You're big buddies now?

FRANK: He's from the government!

EMMA: What government?

FRANK: Our government.

EMMA: I don't know what our government is anymore. Do you? What does that mean, "our government"?

FRANK: That means he knows more than us. He's smarter than us. He knows the big picture, Emma. He's got a plan.

EMMA: What big picture is that?

FRANK: The Enemy. He knows who the Enemy is.

EMMA: What enemy?

(FRANK *hobbles painfully, bowlegged, over toward the basement stairs.*)

FRANK: Where's Graig? Have you seen him?

EMMA: Why are you walking like that?

FRANK: Where's Graig!?

EMMA: I have no idea.

FRANK: (*yelling downstairs*) Graig!!

EMMA: What in the world has gotten into you, Frank?

FRANK: You don't have the slightest clue what's going on here, do you, Emma? We've been infiltrated!

EMMA: What?

(FRANK *begins cruising the rooms suspiciously, looking into corners, behind the plants.*)

FRANK: Targeted. We're in the crosshairs right now, as we speak. Any second now the plants could blow up. The windows shattered.

EMMA: The plants?

FRANK: The milking parlor! The barn! The tractor!

EMMA: The tractor?

FRANK: The manure spreader! The whole kitchen could explode!

EMMA: Stop it!

FRANK: You don't want to hear about it, do you, Emma? You'd much rather go on thinking it's just the two of us, lost out here in an ocean of snow and ice. Milk and cheese. One monotonous frozen day after another.

EMMA: I'm perfectly happy out here.

FRANK: Where is Graig!?

EMMA: I told you, I don't know. Last time I saw him he went down in the basement. Why are you walking like that?

FRANK: I'm in pain!

(*He goes to sofa and collapses. Pause.* EMMA *goes to him.*)

EMMA: Frank, what happened? What have they done to you?

(EMMA *bends down and touches* FRANK'*s shoulder, and a blue flash of light comes from him.* EMMA *screams and jumps back.*)

FRANK: Don't touch me! I'm contaminated!

EMMA: What?

FRANK: You didn't believe that static shock business, did you? He's a carrier. He was sent here to do us in.

EMMA: Sent here? Who would have sent him? I thought he was your friend?

FRANK: He's a traitor! He's betrayed us all. A pretender. They look like us. They act like us. But underneath they're deadly.

(EMMA *rushes over to the potted plants and starts pushing them toward the door. She stacks them all up against the door to block it.*)

What're you doing?

EMMA: (*as she works*) Nobody's getting in here anymore. Nobody!

FRANK: There's going to be a meeting, Emma. Tuesday.

EMMA: No meeting! No Mr. Welch! No Mr. Haynes! Nobody! We are closing our doors to the outside world! I don't care if they set fire to Lake Michigan! This house is closed!

FRANK: You can't stop them.

EMMA: (*still working*) That's the whole trouble—the open-door policy. The friendly neighbor—the borrowing salt and sugar. All that's gonna end. I can't believe you'd sell us down the river like this, Frank! I can't believe it.

FRANK: What?

EMMA: For a bunch of heifers! What'd he give you for those heifers, anyway?

FRANK: (*still on couch*) It's not that. It's not that so much.

EMMA: Well, what is it then? You were happy with those heifers, Frank. We were both happy with those heifers. Now they're gone! For what?

FRANK: For what they are going to contribute to the future security of this nation, Emma!

(EMMA *stops cold, stares at him.*)

EMMA: What?

FRANK: You heard me.

EMMA: Heifers? How are heifers going to contribute to the national security?

FRANK: You'll see. It's all going to be revealed at the meeting. You're going to be very proud of those heifers, Emma. I guarantee you.

EMMA: (*charging* FRANK) There's not going to be any meeting!!!

FRANK: Don't touch me!!

(*A piercing scream from* HAYNES *comes from the basement.* EMMA *and* FRANK *freeze. Long pause.*)

EMMA: (*heavy whisper*) What was that?

FRANK: Don't go down there.

EMMA: I'm not going down there.

FRANK: It's a trap.

EMMA: Frank—how did this happen? How could this be happening to us? We were living so—

FRANK: We weren't paying attention, Emma. We let things slip right past us. I should've known the minute he called me from Rocky Buttes—

EMMA: Don't say that name!

FRANK: What?

EMMA: That name—you shouldn't be tossing that around. It's top secret.

FRANK: Is that what he told you?

EMMA: Who?

FRANK: Graig.

EMMA: I thought he was your friend.

FRANK: So did I.

EMMA: Maybe they're in this together—the two of them. A conspiracy.

FRANK: No.

EMMA: Why not? He sends Haynes out here to soften us up; then he steps in for the kill.

FRANK: Kill? Who? Mr. Welch?

EMMA: Yes.

FRANK: Mr. Welch is a righteous man!

(*Another sharp scream from* HAYNES *out of the basement.* FRANK *and* EMMA *freeze.*)

EMMA: One of us has to go down there.

FRANK: That's just what they want, Emma. That's exactly what they want.

EMMA: They? See—how many of them are there?

FRANK: I don't know.

EMMA: It sounds like he's being tortured.

FRANK: He's used to that.

EMMA: I'm going down there!

FRANK: No!

(FRANK *grabs her but lets go immediately as another bolt of light comes from his arm. Pause.* EMMA *stares at him.*)

EMMA: Frank, the whole world can't just suddenly get turned inside out like this overnight.

(*The sounds of heavy, labored breathing, feet scraping against the basement staircase; a low moaning comes from basement.* EMMA *and* FRANK *stare in that direction. Slowly,* WELCH *appears in shirtsleeves coming up the stairs backward, pulling on a long black electrical cord apparently tied to something heavy at the bottom of the stairs.*)

WELCH: (*breathing heavily, pulling on cord*) This—this is what we're up against now, Frank. Lying, deception, manipulating the truth! Right here in your own home. Right down in your own basement! A man who claims to be your friend. An ally. Can you believe it? There he was, hovering down there in a corner, plotting your annihilation. I finally got it out of him. Got to the nasty rock bottom of it.

EMMA: You're not torturing him, are you? What're you doing?

WELCH: Torturing? Torturing! We're not in a Third World nation here, Emma. This isn't some dark corner of the Congo. Frank, haven't you told her about our new platform? Our design for the new century?

EMMA: (*moving toward stairs*) What are you doing to Mr. Haynes?

WELCH: Haynes? That's not his name, Emma. That never was his name. That's just a cover so he can sneak around and deceive innocent people like you and Frank.

(WELCH *punches a button attached to the black cord.* HAYNES *yells out in pain from below.* EMMA *runs to top of stairs and looks down.*)

EMMA: Oh, my God! Frank! He's got him by the penis!

(FRANK *stands suddenly on couch, grabbing his own crotch.*)

FRANK: What?

EMMA: Come and look! He's got that cord attached to his penis. (*to* WELCH, *charging him, hitting his shoulders*) You stop that right now! Just stop it!

(WELCH *pushes her away roughly, keeps ahold of cord.* FRANK *keeps standing on couch, holding his crotch.*)

WELCH: Now's not the time for hysterics, Emma. We just fall into their game plan that way. Isn't that right, Frank? Isn't that what we discussed? I'm surprised you haven't had a chance to talk things over with Emma.

EMMA: Stop calling me by my name! I hate that!

WELCH: She needs to get on the same page. Stop acting like some whacked-out subversive. You've explained the dangers to her, haven't you? Frank? The folly of mixed messages?

FRANK: (*still on couch, holding crotch*) She doesn't know a thing.

EMMA: What don't I know?

WELCH: Well, we've got to get her involved, Frank. She can't be flopping around on the outside of the loop, like a fish outa water. It's too risky.

EMMA: What don't I know!? What don't I know!? That's what I want to know!

WELCH: Let's get your pal Haynes up here. See what kind of a mood he's in now. Maybe he's ready to shed some light on the whole project. What do you say, Emma?

(WELCH *punches the buttons on the remote control.* HAYNES *screams from below.*)

EMMA: Stop doing that! That's got to be hurting—

WELCH: Sounds like he might be ready to give us a few clues. (*yelling down to* HAYNES *as he hauls him up with cord*) Come on up here now! Front and center, Mr. "Haynes."

(*A scream from* HAYNES *as* WELCH *hauls him to the top of the stairs and into the room.* HAYNES *comes crashing up, clutching the black cord with both hands. The cord runs directly into the fly of* HAYNES*'s pants.* HAYNES *is now in T-shirt, bare feet, and old khaki pants. He wears a black hood on his head. He stands there panting.* WELCH *rips the hood off.* EMMA—*off to the side, horrified.* FRANK *stays standing on couch, staring out at audience and clutching his crotch.*)

(*holding cord*) There we go! Finally, we have arrived! Haven't we, Haynes? Debriefed, recoded, resurfaced, and good to go!

EMMA: (*to* WELCH) Is that attached to his penis? Is that cord actually attached—

WELCH: Well, we don't want to give away too many secrets, do we, Emma? These techniques are well guarded—

EMMA: Because if that is attached to his—thing, then there's no question that this is torture! This is absolute torture! I don't care what country we're in.

WELCH: (*offering cord to* EMMA) Would you like to hold him for a little while, Emma?

EMMA: (*backing away*) No! No, I would *not* like to hold him.

WELCH: It's just like holding the leash of a well-behaved dog.

EMMA: Frank!

WELCH: Exactly the same.

EMMA: Frank! Snap out of it!

FRANK: (*out to audience again*) It's times like this you remember the world was perfect once. Absolutely perfect. Powder blue skies. Hawks circling over the bottom fields. The rich smell of fresh-cut alfalfa laying in lazy wind rows. The gentle bawling of spring calves calling to their mothers. I miss the Cold War so much.

WELCH: (*to* HAYNES) Sit!

(WELCH *punches a button on the remote control and* HAYNES *immediately goes to his knees like a trained dog.*)

Now, Frank—turn around and say hello to your old compadre.

FRANK: (*stays standing on couch, facing audience*) He is no compadre of mine. He's a two-faced, camel-loving—

WELCH: Now, now—we mustn't judge him too harshly. We're all guilty of a little backsliding from time to time. A little left-leaning—

EMMA: (*to* WELCH) Could I get him some water at least?

WELCH: Of course.

(EMMA *goes to sink, gets water.* HAYNES, *on his knees, starts ranting as* EMMA *brings water back to him.*)

HAYNES: (*on knees*) This is that moment—that place in time. You remember—there were these—there are, now—history. This is it now. Where we move—where we—we must—seize the day. That's it! We must—snap ourselves back into it. Grab ahold. Jump right in there and smash the holy shit out of them before they get any more smart-ass ideas. This is it! We must—don't you know that? Don't you know?

EMMA: What in the world is he saying?

WELCH: He's just reprogramming, Emma. He'll be fine. Up now, Haynes! On your feet! Front and center. Do the step. Look lively. Let's see it. The step! The step! Do the step!

(WELCH *snaps the cord.* HAYNES *lets out a short yell, scrambles to his feet, and starts marching in place in some weird cadenced step.* EMMA *backs away with the glass of water.*)

Time to get down to brass tacks here. Now, explain to Frank exactly what we have in mind here, Haynes. Everything we've gone through down in the basement. Our little ordeal. Come on, speak up, speak up! Don't be shy.

(HAYNES *staggers forward and speaks with some difficulty. He stops marching for a second.*)

Don't give up the step, Haynes! We've got to maintain at all costs! The step! The step! There you go. Now tell Frank. Go ahead.

(HAYNES *picks up the march again and speaks to* FRANK.)

HAYNES: (*marching*) We're—what they want us to do—what they want is—we're supposed to head back there. All the way back. At night—by train—(*to* WELCH) Isn't that it? Am I on the right track?

WELCH: That's it! That's it! Keep going—keep in step! Give him a little water, Emma. Just a dribble.

FRANK: Train? By train? What the heck is he saying?

(EMMA *gives* HAYNES *a small sip, then backs away.* HAYNES *stops marching for a second.* WELCH *is on him.*)

WELCH: Keep it up! Keep it up! The step, the step!

(HAYNES *resumes his little march in place.*)

HAYNES: We're supposed to head back with the heifers. At night. By train. Across the Great Plains. The two of us.

FRANK: Me? Not me.

HAYNES: Me and you both. Across the Great Plains. Clack-ety clack.

FRANK: No! That couldn't be right. I'm supposed to be at the meeting!

WELCH: Where, though, Haynes? Where exactly is "back there"? Be specific. Frank needs to know. You can do it. You're a big boy. Tell Frank.

(WELCH *zaps him with electric shock. Blue light.*)

HAYNES: ROCKY BUTTES!!!!!

WELCH: There we go. That wasn't so hard, now, was it?

FRANK: Rocky Buttes? I thought you told me they were going to be air-dropped into exotic foreign lands. That's what you said. Palm trees! Desert oasis! Parachutes floating!

WELCH: You just keep dreaming, Frank.

EMMA: How are you going to explain Holsteins in the middle of the desert?

WELCH: They snuck in from Canada. It doesn't matter.

FRANK: You told me my heifers were going to be glorified. Heroic!

WELCH: You've got to drop all that for now, Frank. Leave the simple past behind. We've got to get a move on here. We're dealing with a ruthless, diabolical, treacherous, despicable force. What's the matter with you people? Don't you get it?

FRANK: No, this isn't what I had in mind. You painted me a different picture. (*coming down off sofa, tries to hand case back to* WELCH) Here, you take this money back. I don't want it.

WELCH: Too late for that, Frank. Way too late.

FRANK: Take it back!

(FRANK *opens case and empties the money out.*)

WELCH: Things have already been set in motion. There's no more thinking to do. It's time for action. Look at your friend, Haynes. How committed he is. You don't want to be left behind, do you, Frank? Out here in the hinterlands. Get in step! Get in step!

(HAYNES *keeps up his marching, getting more and more frantic, as* FRANK *looks on.*)

Things are going to start moving very, very fast now. Everything's been building to this. You'll see. The wonderful part is that the machinery is in place! All we have to do is climb on board now, Frank. Take a ride!

We are going to deliver you to your Manifest Destiny! Just take a little test-drive. Get in step, Frank. Try it out.

(FRANK *starts tentatively marching with* HAYNES, *trying to fall into step with him, but* HAYNES *has now cranked up the tempo.* FRANK *tries to catch up.*)

Emma, maybe you could clean the place up a bit. Get these plants out of here before the meeting.

EMMA: Frank! Frank, don't do that. Stop doing that!

WELCH: I've got all my people coming, Emma. What are they going to think about our readiness? We've got to get the place cleaned up.

(FRANK *keeps on marching with* HAYNES; *the two of them getting more and more in sync.* . . . EMMA *rushes to* FRANK *and grabs his arm, trying to stop him from marching with* HAYNES. *Blue light flashes from* FRANK's *arm.* EMMA *jumps back.*)

EMMA: (*grabbing* FRANK, *who continues marching*) Frank! Stop it now! This isn't you! This isn't who you are! Frank! What have they done to you!?

(FRANK *and* HAYNES *keep marching in unison.* WELCH *takes each of them by the arm and leads them toward the door, knocking over plants on the way.*)

WELCH: You're going to like Rocky Buttes, Frank. Whole different landscape. Wide open. Just like the Wild, Wild West. Not a tree in sight. Endlessly flat and lifeless.

(WELCH *opens door and escorts* HAYNES *and* FRANK *out to the porch.* EMMA *stands in the room, helpless.*)

FRANK: Have they got any pasture out there, Graig?

HAYNES: Buffalo grass. That's about it.

FRANK: How are we going to feed my heifers?

WELCH: Just keep making your way down across those frozen fields. My people will pick you up on the road. You see the headlights? They're waiting for you. Keep in step now. Don't forget to keep in step.

(FRANK *and* HAYNES *go off past the windows, maintaining their little pathetic march.* WELCH *comes back into the house and speaks to* EMMA.)

(*to* EMMA) Well, don't act so surprised, Emma. What did you expect? You didn't think you were going to get a free ride on the back of Democracy forever, did you? Well, did you? What have you done to deserve such rampant freedom? Such total lack of responsibility. Just lolling about here in the Wisconsin wilderness with your useless lumberjack of a husband, scraping the cream off the countryside. Sooner or later, the price has to be paid. Don't you think? Our day has come. Now, be a good girl and clean the place up for our meeting. We need to put our best foot forward, don't we? Get in step, Emma. Get in step. See you Tuesday.

(WELCH *turns and goes out the door, closing it behind him. He disappears past the windows. Pause.* EMMA *turns toward audience and walks extreme downstage, staring out. She just stands there, staring.*)

EMMA: (*to herself*) Frank.

(*She just stands there awhile, then turns and runs upstage, goes out door, leaving it open, and starts ringing the bell. She keeps ringing it as the lights fade. As lights get dimmer, the plants begin to emanate blue flashes, which increase in intensity as lights go to black. Music over. Bell continues.*)

END

ALSO BY SAM SHEPARD

CRUISING PARADISE
Tales

A boy travels to a roadside inn to retrieve the mattress on which his drunken father burned to death. A mortified actor bulldozes his way through the Mexican border bureaucracy by pretending to be Spencer Tracy. A man and a woman quarrel desperately in a South Dakota motel room and part company for reasons neither can understand. The stories in *Cruising Paradise* map the places where our culture is defined, from a writer who has become synonymous with the recklessness, stoicism, and solitude of American manhood.

Fiction/Short Stories/0-679-74217-4

GREAT DREAM OF HEAVEN
Stories

A woman driving her mother's ashes across the country has a strangely transcendent run-in with an injured hawk. Two aging widowers, in Stetsons and bolo ties, together make a daily pilgrimage to the local Denny's, only to be divided by the attentions of their favorite waitress. A boy watches a "remedy man" tame a wild stallion, a contest that mirrors his own struggle with his father. Peering unblinkingly into the chasms that separate fathers and sons, husbands and wives, friends and strangers, these lyrical tales bear the unmistakable signature of an American master.

Fiction/Short Stories/0-375-70452-3

SIMPATICO
A Play

Carter ought to be managing his thoroughbred business in Kentucky. Instead, he is in a room in Cucamonga, Nowheresville, U.S.A., trying to get back in the good graces of Vinnie, the one man who has the power to destroy him. From the beginning, Sam Shepard's *Simpatico* launches us into the world of horse racing, where high society meets the low life and the line between winners and losers is as treacherously thin as a razor blade.

Drama/0-679-76317-1

THE LATE HENRY MOSS, EYES FOR CONSUELA, WHEN THE WORLD WAS GREEN
Three Plays

In *The Late Henry Moss*, two estranged brothers confront the past as they piece together the drunken fishing expedition that preceded their father's death. In *Eyes for Consuela*, a vacationing American encounters a knife-toting Mexican bandit on a gruesome quest. And in *When the World Was Green*, a journalist in search of her father interviews an old man who resolved a vendetta by murdering the wrong man.

Drama/1-4000-3079-X

STATES OF SHOCK, FAR NORTH, SILENT TONGUE
A Play and Two Screenplays

Sam Shepard's writing tears through the envelope between prose and poetry and between pop culture and myth. In the play *States of Shock*, a nostalgic colonel and his mutilated guest celebrate a bizarre anniversary—and in the process reopen the wounds of war, sexuality, and familial betrayal. The screenplay *Far North* looks fondly across the gap of gender and generation. And in his screenplay *Silent Tongue*, Shepard turns the history of the white presence on the frontier into something resembling Greek tragedy.

Drama/0-679-74218-2

THE UNSEEN HAND
And Other Plays

If you visit Sam Shepard country, expect to find bayous, deserts, and junkyards where dreams rust alongside abandoned Chevys. Prepare to meet broken gunmen, refugees from distant galaxies, slavering swamp things, and California highway patrolmen. Sam Shepard does nothing less than renew America's myths—and sometimes he invents them from scratch. In these fourteen works for the theater, our most audacious living playwright sets genres and archetypes spinning, with utterly mesmerizing results.

Drama/0-679-76789-4

VINTAGE BOOKS
Available at your local bookstore, or call toll-free to order:
1-800-793-2665 (credit cards only).